I0180594

GRACE, GRATITUDE, AND GIVING

GRACE, GRATITUDE, AND GIVING

BIBLICAL REFLECTIONS ON

CHRISTIAN PHILANTHROPY

Edited by Jeffrey P. Greenman

REGENT COLLEGE PUBLISHING
Vancouver, British Columbia

Grace, Gratitude, and Giving
Copyright © 2020 Jeffrey P. Greenman

Regent College Publishing
5800 University Boulevard
Vancouver, BC V6T 2E4 Canada

All rights reserved. No part of this publication may be reproduced, stored in a retrieval system, or transmitted, in any form or by any means, electronic, mechanical, photocopying, recording or otherwise, without the prior written permission of the author, except in the case of brief quotations embodied in critical articles and reviews.

Regent College Publishing is an imprint of the Regent Bookstore (RegentBookstore.com). Views expressed in works published by Regent College Publishing are those of the author and do not necessarily represent the official position of Regent College (Regent-College.edu).

ISBN: 978-1-57383-591-6

Unless otherwise noted, all Scripture citations in this volume are from the New International Version (NIV).

To the generous financial supporters of Regent College,
past, present, and future

CONTENTS

Editor's Preface by Jeffrey P. Greenman / 1

1. The Heart of the Matter (Exodus 35:4–9, 20–29)
   Jeffrey P. Greenman / 5
2. Participating in the Emergence of God's New
   Creation (Exodus 3:1–15)
   Christie Goode / 19
3. It's All Gift (Psalms 111–112)
   Richard Thompson / 32
4. The Unfortunate Case of the Uncheerful Giver
   (Mark 12:41–44)
   Jeffrey P. Greenman / 45
5. The Conversion of the Wallet
   (2 Corinthians 9:1–15)
   Rod J. K. Wilson / 57
6. From Money to Doxology (Philippians 4:10–20)
   Nicole Den Haan / 69
7. Always, Everything, and Whatever
   (1 Thessalonians 5:16–18; Philippians 4:4–6;
   Colossians 3:15–17)
   Stephen W. T. Stinton / 84

Further Reading / 97
Contributors / 99

EDITOR'S PREFACE

Jeffrey P. Greenman

This book is a modest attempt to deepen the conversation among Christians about our relationship to money and the idea of giving some of it away—a subject usually considered awkward at best, and perhaps even off-limits in many church circles.

It is intended to assist Christian lay people and pastors alike to gain some valuable glimpses into the Bible's way of thinking about money, possessions, and generosity. These chapters aim to help Christians give fresh attention to our beliefs, attitudes, and behaviours related to what we do with money. We hope that it will stimulate our thinking about the foundational beliefs underpinning the practices of Christian philanthropy.

We write for the ordinary reader, not the academic specialist. This volume does not provide a full or systematic account of money, possessions, and giving in the Bible. That would require a much longer volume from accomplished biblical scholars.

Rather than attempting comprehensive coverage of the numerous important texts related to our central themes, we offer a selective sampling from both Old and New Testaments. We provide seven sermons on some passages that have struck us as poignant, particularly ones which illuminate the theological-spiritual intersection of grace, gratitude, and generosity. They retain their character as actual, real-life sermons—more informal in style and more personal in approach than what you would find in an academic essay.

Our intention in incorporating Scripture texts is to highlight the primacy of the Bible's own words, which our authors' words seek to illuminate and to serve, in order that our readers might (in the words of an Anglican prayer) "read, mark, learn, and inwardly digest" the Bible's message on these important themes.

We would be pleased if these biblical reflections could be a helpful resource for pastors as they prepare their own sermons, for Bible study or discussion groups, and for prayerful consideration by individuals or families as they consider their stewardship. We also hope that the book could strength and support professionals in the field of Christian philanthropy.

The chapters are authored by six people who share a deep connection to the ministry of Regent College in Vancouver, British Columbia, Canada. All six have been thoroughly involved in Regent's fundraising work. Most of these sermons were given either in the context of Regent's chapel services or when someone has served as a guest preacher in a congregation, having been asked to preach on the theme of stewardship. Five are Regent alumni; the only non-alumnus is a former Regent president.

Ultimately, we offer this book in the hope that, as an expression of Regent's core mission, it might be used by God "to cultivate intelligent, vigorous and joyful commitment to Jesus Christ, his church and his world."

1

THE HEART OF THE MATTER

Exodus 35:4–9, 20–29

Jeffrey P. Greenman

On a number of occasions, I've been asked by pastors to give a "stewardship" message in their church. Usually this invitation comes during their "stewardship month," which focuses on securing pledges or "commitments" from parishioners for their donations during the upcoming year. Usually this is accompanied by a presentation of the church budget, with its nitty-gritty details of how much it will cost to keep the lights on. Seeing as their own salaries are paid by church revenues, some pastors are quite uncomfortable with preaching in this context. At best, it's a bit awkward, akin to singing for your supper. At worst, it's felt to be self-serving and therefore improper. A neutral outsider, such as an innocent visitor, is sometimes freer to speak honestly to the congregation about their financial giving.

I welcome the opportunity to speak to congregations about their "stewardship." After all, the concept of stewardship is expansive. How God's people should wisely care for our entire relationship to God's world and handle our portion of God-given resources is a major concern throughout the entire Bible. Too often these matters are neglected or marginalized. An important part of the broader question of stewardship undoubtedly is what we are doing with our money, which is usually a taboo subject, and whether we are willing to give it away. Strangely enough, in many North American churches, and perhaps also elsewhere, there is only one Sunday every year when we can speak directly about money.

Speaking of taboo subjects, we should remember that Jesus talked far more about money than he did about sex. He also talked about money more often than about prayer or faith. About one-quarter of his parables were about money or possessions. His keen interest in this topic might puzzle us. Why did he devote so much time to this theme? I would suggest that his interest stems from the insight that what we do with our money, better than anything else, reveals the spiritual condition of our hearts. "For where your treasure is, there your heart will be also" (Luke 12:34). The connection between our treasure and our hearts is a deep theme of the Old Testament, which is precisely where Jesus would have learned it.

GOD'S GENEROUS PROVISION IN EXODUS

To explore this theme, there are many Old Testament passages that we could examine. I believe the core narrative about generous giving in the Old Testament is the story of the construction of the tabernacle in the book of Exodus.

The book of Exodus is famous for its remarkably dramatic stories:

- God encountering Moses at the burning bush, with the revelation of God's identity as "I am who I am"
- Moses' confrontation with the Egyptian Pharaoh and the horrifying plagues
- God's deliverance of the Israelites in the exodus through a miraculous escape through the sea
- the provision of manna in the wilderness
- God's giving of the Torah, including Ten Commandments, on Mount Sinai
- covenant ratification between God and his people

All this is covered in the first twenty-four chapters. These are some of the most important and memorable events in the Bible.

Usually our interest as readers (or preachers) tails off considerably when it comes to Exodus 25–40, however. Sermon series and Bible studies often conclude with chapter 24, or even chapter 20. After all, virtually all the material found in chapters 25–40 deals with the detailed instructions for and the construction of the tabernacle in the wilderness. We are tempted to wonder why this sort of boring historical stuff is there. Can we just skim over this quickly and move on to more interesting texts? Ho-hum? Actually, no. We are unwise to skip or skate over it quickly, especially if our interest is in the question of how God's people handled their money and possessions.

Before we look at what happens in Exodus 25 onward—and zoom in on chapter 35 in particular—we need to remind ourselves of some usually overlooked features of the first twenty-four chapters that set the stage for some remarkable action by the Israelites in these allegedly boring chapters.

The story of God's grace and provision for his people permeates the entire narrative. There are clear previews of what God's people will do which are fulfilled later in the story. In Exodus 3, after God encounters Moses at the burning bush, God is preparing

Moses for his own encounter with the king of Egypt, explaining what will happen. Looking ahead to their escape from Egypt, we read: "And I will make the Egyptians favorably disposed toward this people, so that when you leave you will not go empty-handed. Every woman is to ask her neighbor and any woman living in her house for articles of silver and gold and for clothing, which you will put on your sons and daughters. And so you will plunder the Egyptians" (3:21–22). The text is telling us how God will provide for his people as they are delivered from bondage and set off into freedom in wilderness. It testifies to God's grace.

The description of God's chosen means of provision is basically repeated in Exodus 11:2–3, amidst the story of the plagues: "'Tell the people that men and women alike are to ask their neighbors for articles of silver and gold.' (The Lord made the Egyptians favorably disposed toward the people, and Moses himself was highly regarded in Egypt by Pharaoh's officials and by the people.)"

Finally, the great moment of escape comes. Part of the miracle of the exodus is the Lord's provision through the Egyptians: "The Israelites did as Moses instructed and asked the Egyptians for articles of silver and gold and for clothing. The Lord had made the Egyptians favorably disposed toward the people, and they gave them what they asked for; so they plundered the Egyptians" (12:35–36).

The English word *plunder* (Hebrew *natsal*) used here carries very negative connotations. Plundering or "despoiling" means stealing, taking by force what is not yours. Jewish and Christian commentators have struggled with this passage for centuries. Yet the text emphasizes that the Egyptians gave over their possessions willingly and freely to the Israelites because God moved in the situation to make them "favorably disposed" to do so. Perhaps a translation more like "they stripped the Egyptians of their goods" would be better.

As usual in the Bible, and most certainly in the book of Exodus, the main actor on the stage is God himself. On account of divine action on the Israelites' behalf, the action in this scene is not the same thing as having those goods taken away by force. The end result for the Egyptians was effectively their "plundering" in the sense that their goods were removed from Egypt. The end result for the Israelites is that they did not leave empty-handed but with God-appointed gifts for their journey. I suggest that this episode taught the Israelites that their God was a God of abundant, caring provision—a lesson reinforced as their journey unfolded. In so providing for his people, God enabled them to become generous givers when the occasion required.

As their journey continues, God delivers the Israelites "with a mighty hand" as they cross over the Red Sea on dry ground (Exodus 14). This demonstrates the incomparable power and glory of God (Exodus 15). Quickly we find the Israelites "grumbling" against Moses and Aaron in the desert (16:2). God responds with the gift of manna to feed them, which becomes their daily food for forty years (16:35). Surely the lesson here again was that their God was a generous God who provides abundantly. He could be trusted to sustain his people. They could depend upon God for all their needs.

In Exodus 19–24, the people come to Mount Sinai, the place of God's revelation of the Torah. Here we learn that the Israelites are to be a "kingdom of priests and a holy nation" (19:24), set apart for a special relationship with God himself. That special relationship is marked by a remarkable covenant ratification celebratory meal at which the leaders of Israel "saw God, and they ate and drank" (24:11). The grace of God is again evident, this time in a welcoming invitation to divine fellowship.

GENEROUS GOD, GENEROUS PEOPLE

This brings us, finally, to Exodus 25. My point in recounting this history is that we need to recall that God had provided generously and abundantly for them throughout the story so far. In order for what we read in Exodus 25 to make sense, we need to remember that God blessed the Israelites in the exodus through the gracious gift of the "plundering," and in the wilderness wanderings through the gracious gift of the manna, and through the gift of Torah at Mount Sinai.

In Exodus 25 we find ourselves face to face with the first fundraising project in the Bible. The goal is to build a tabernacle or sanctuary, where God will dwell, and provide for priestly garments and sacred furnishings, which requires various materials: "The LORD said to Moses, 'Tell the Israelites to bring me an offering. You are to receive the offering for me from everyone whose heart prompts them to give'" (25:2). This verse sets the entire biblical trajectory about financial giving by God's people. It is hard to overestimate its importance for our understanding of grace, gratitude, and generosity. The elements are quite distinctive.

First, notice that the Lord says that the Israelites are to "bring me an offering." This is giving to God himself. Even today when we speak about "giving to the church," we need to remember that, first and foremost, our giving is to God.

Second, we must not miss that the Israelites are to give freely. It is a free will offering, not a mandatory tax payment. There is no hint of compulsion here.

Third, their giving is described as a matter of heart. Only those whose hearts "prompt" or motivate them to give should do so. We may be surprised to find that there is no sense of obligation or duty involved. It is a matter of choice, and beyond that, a matter of desire. There is no sense here that they are giving to God in order to earn his favour or to benefit themselves.

Fourth, everyone is invited to participate. No one is excluded. All are included equally in the opportunity. Presumably some would give larger amounts, others would give smaller amounts.

The text then moves directly into the elaborate details of construction of the sanctuary. The flow of the narrative appears to be interrupted by the story of the golden calf in chapter 32. An interesting detail of that account is their apparent enthusiasm for giving: "Aaron answered them, 'Take off the gold earrings that your wives, your sons and your daughters are wearing, and bring them to me.' So all the people took off their earrings and brought them to Aaron" (32:2–3). Again, what were they giving to the construction of the golden calf? The gold jewelry they acquired in Egypt through God's provision for them in the "plundering" upon departure. Whatever they had to give (toward making an idol) can only have been what they had received from the Lord. Their giving was misguided, but it was quite generous.

And who was their divine provider? Even in the aftermath of the idolatrous debacle of the golden calf, God revealed himself as a gracious God, who is "The LORD, the LORD, the compassionate and gracious God, slow to anger, abounding in love and faithfulness, maintaining love to thousands, and forgiving wickedness, rebellion and sin. Yet he does not leave the guilty unpunished; he punishes the children and their children for the sin of the parents to the third and fourth generation" (34:6–7).

With the detailed instructions about the tabernacle construction spelled out, it was time for the work to begin. Thus, we read in Exodus 35:4–9:

> Moses said to the whole Israelite community, "This is what the LORD has commanded: From what you have, take an offering for the LORD. Everyone who is willing is to bring to the LORD an offering of gold, silver and bronze; blue, purple and scarlet yarn and fine linen; goat hair; ram skins dyed red and another type of durable leather; acacia wood; olive oil for the light; spices for the anointing oil and for the fragrant incense; and

onyx stones and other gems to be mounted on the ephod and breastpiece.

The key here is verse 5, which has also been translated: "Take from among you a contribution to the LORD. Whoever is of a generous heart, let him bring the LORD's contribution" (ESV).

There is nothing forced or grudging about their giving. As in Exodus 25:2, the emphasis is on giving only from those who are willing. The only kind of giving imagined is voluntary.

Then, after Moses invites skilled workmen to come forward to make everything the Lord has commanded, we read, "the whole Israelite community withdrew from Moses' presence, and everyone who was willing and whose heart moved them came and brought an offering to the LORD for the work on the tent of meeting, for all its service, and for the sacred garments. All who were willing, men and women alike, came and brought gold jewelry of all kinds" (35:20–22).

From the standpoint of a conducting a huge fundraising project, it is interesting that Moses allowed the people to withdraw to consider their involvement in the work. He did not pressure them for an immediate response. Why? Because he knew it was a matter of the heart. A voluntary gift needs to be the fruit of a sincere commitment. There needed to be time and space for consideration or maybe even discussion in family groups. People should give only if their heart "moved them" to bring an offering, not because they felt compelled by their leader to do so.

What is the result? All the Israelite men and women who were willing brought to the Lord freewill offerings for all the work the Lord through Moses had commanded them to do (35:29). Again, we find the clear emphasis on the willingness of people giving freely. Apparently not everyone decided to give. Was that a problem for the community? Apparently not.

The text also tells us that the skilled workers received the offerings that the Israelites continually brought, day after day. Amazingly, the people gave so generously they had to be told to stop. Can you imagine that happening in our churches' fundraising campaigns?

> They received from Moses all the offerings the Israelites had brought to carry out the work of constructing the sanctuary. And the people continued to bring freewill offerings morning after morning. So all the skilled workers who were doing all the work on the sanctuary left what they were doing and said to Moses, "The people are bringing more than enough for doing the work the LORD commanded to be done."

> Then Moses gave an order and they sent this word throughout the camp: "No man or woman is to make anything else as an offering for the sanctuary." And so the people were restrained from bringing more, because what they already had was more than enough to do all the work. (36:3–7)

This is a picture of an extremely generous people. They give freely, willingly, and from the heart—far more than what was needed. Exodus 35 tells us repeatedly that this was the key factor in the project. Verses 5, 21, 22, 26, and 29 refer to the willing hearts of the people. It's hard not to see the point with all this repetition. One way the Hebrew Bible shows us something is important is by sheer repetition. Let's not miss it.

Their generosity made possible the tabernacle, God's dwelling place, which was completed according to God's exact design. We read in Exodus 39:42–43, "The Israelites had done all the work just as the Lord had commanded Moses. Moses inspected the work and saw that they had done it just as the Lord had commanded. So Moses blessed them." With the finishing touches of the work completed, "the glory of the Lord filled the tabernacle" (40:34). God was dwelling with his people.

TO LIVE IS TO GIVE

Commenting on the generosity of the Israelites demonstrated both in the golden calf episode and in the tabernacle project, Rabbi Jonathan Sacks, one of contemporary Judaism's leading thinkers, comments: "In Judaism, to live is to give." Such is the centrality of generosity in their religious identity, past and present.

God's people of the old covenant and new covenant alike are invited to generous giving from the heart. Does our giving come from a willing heart? Or perhaps from other motivations? Are we giving reluctantly or under compulsion? What pleases God are offerings "from everyone whose heart prompts them to give" (Exodus 25:2). We know, too, that the apostle Paul teaches that "each one must give as he has decided in his heart, not reluctantly or under compulsion, for God loves a cheerful giver" (2 Corinthians 9:7). Paul's instruction expresses the same outlook as our foundational Old Testament text about giving that we have been studying together.

May the Lord work in our hearts, by his grace, to prompt us as his grateful people to give generously to his cause in the world, for the sake of his honour and glory.

2

PARTICIPATING IN THE EMERGENCE OF GOD'S NEW CREATION

Exodus 3:1–15

Christie Goode

Last autumn, a seed that had been planted in me by Darrell Johnson some fifteen years ago at Regent began to grow and bud. It was about Moses at the burning bush. You remember that story, right?

What's been growing in me recently is the connection between this burning bush in the ancient desert of northeast Egypt and the infinite density of the universe a nanosecond before the Big Bang. I know—crazy. But unpacking this connection can teach us something vital about our practice of philanthropy today.

THE REVELATION OF GOD'S WITH-NESS AND FOR-NESS

> One day, after Moses had grown up, he went out to where his own people were and watched them at their hard labor. He saw an Egyptian beating a Hebrew, one of his own people. Looking this way and that and seeing no one, he killed the Egyptian and hid him in the sand. The next day he went out and saw two Hebrews fighting. He asked the one in the wrong, "Why are you hitting your fellow Hebrew?" (Exodus 2:11–13)

Let's start with Moses, who has impulsively murdered an Egyptian man to protect a Hebrew slave. He discovers that the news is spreading. On top of that, it seems the Hebrews don't care two whits that he was trying to protect them. Pharaoh finds out and tries to kill him, so he flees to Midian.

Many years later, as recorded in Exodus 3, Moses is tending sheep near Mount Sinai and he sees a bush that is engulfed in flames but doesn't burn up. That's curious. So he approaches.

> Now Moses was tending the flock of Jethro his father-in-law, the priest of Midian, and he led the flock to the far side of the wilderness and came to Horeb, the mountain of God. There the angel of the LORD appeared to him in flames of fire from

> within a bush. Moses saw that though the bush
> was on fire it did not burn up. So Moses thought,
> "I will go over and see this strange sight—why the
> bush does not burn up." (vv. 1–3)

A messenger of the LORD speaks to him through
the burning bush and gives him a new mission: to go
back to Egypt, talk to Pharaoh, and lead the Hebrews
out of Egypt, where they'd been living for four hundred years. Yeah, right. The text reads:

> But Moses said to God, "Who am I that I should go
> to Pharaoh and bring the Israelites out of Egypt?"
> And God said, "I will be with you. And this will
> be the sign to you that it is I who have sent you:
> When you have brought the people out of Egypt,
> you will worship God on this mountain."
>
> Moses said to God, "Suppose I go to the Isra-
> elites and say to them, 'The God of your fathers
> has sent me to you,' and they ask me, 'What is his
> name?' Then what shall I tell them?" (vv. 11–13)

Not surprisingly, part of Moses' response (v. 13)
to this voice from the bush was, "Um . . . this is cool
and all . . . pretty amazing, actually, but . . . which
god are you? When I tell these hundreds of thousands
of slaves to follow me, who exactly should I say is
leading us to freedom?"

The voice in the bush replies, "Yahweh" (v. 14). The NIV says: God said to Moses, "I AM WHO I AM. This is what you are to say to the Israelites: 'I AM has sent me to you.'" The name Yahweh is usually translated as "I am who I am." Furthermore, the voice said, "This is my name forever, the name you shall call me from generation to generation" (v. 15).

God reveals his name. And in the ancient world, one's name revealed one's character, so by revealing his name, God was revealing something core about his character. His essence. I am Yahweh. The Hebrews valued this revelation so tenderly that through the centuries they developed customs to avoid saying the word *Yahweh*, lest it inadvertently be spoken without proper reverence and respect.

"Yahweh" is a precious revelation.

But what does it mean? We have become so comfortable with the translation of "I am who I am" that we rarely give it a second thought. And in our individualist society, it's easy and natural to assume it means "I am God and I can be whoever I want to be, and you have no right or power to question it." I am who I am.

But the seed that Darrell Johnson planted in me, which has recently started to grow, was a deeper explanation of what the word *Yahweh* actually means.

It's a form of the Hebrew verb for "to be." In Western culture, we interpret that in an existential sense—"to be or not to be." But in the Hebrew, it is "to be" with a sense of presence. Concordances give the meaning of the word as "fall out" or "come to pass" or "become."

Darrell said his best definition was "to be with and for." Presence and solidarity are implicit, along with a trajectory of support. God's very essence, his character that defines him, that names him, is a deep with-ness and for-ness.

THE EMERGENCE OF CREATION

The wonderful new connection (for me) has been to realize that Yahweh's revelation that his name/character/essence is with-ness and for-ness fits perfectly with our scientific, cosmological understanding of life in our universe.

Scientists tell us now, as generally accepted fact, that the universe began about 13.8 billion years ago, perhaps as a singularity, which is a location in space-time of infinite density. All the matter of the universe may have existed together, in one infinitesimal space-moment. Since then, the universe has been constantly expanding. For 13.8 billion years, the space between every point in the universe has been constantly expanding. This is called omnicentricity—all

23

points began in a centre and constantly expand equally away from a centre, such that any of the points can at any time be considered the centre.

The Scriptures tell us that God is the Alpha and the Omega. He is the beginning and the end. He is the energizing creative force behind all things, holding all things together. Viewing God through this lens of physics makes sense when paired with God's self-revelation that he is Yahweh—he is the very foundational force of with-ness and for-ness.

With-ness: in such solidarity, in such constant and cohabitating presence to the degree of the entire universe being held in one space-moment.

For-ness: with such loving trajectory, using that with-ness in support of new creation that is constantly emerging. New creation in every moment, in every direction, that constantly expands the universe.

How does this happen? How could the breath-Spirit of Yahweh, how could the character of with-ness and for-ness, become a constantly expanding universe of stars and planets and creatures and plants and humans and relationships and the daily chore of feeding your daughter's guinea pig?

Emergence.

Emergence is the scientific phenomenon of a new quality emerging out of massive quantity. It's when a collective entity is observed to have properties its individual parts do not have on their own. These properties or behaviors emerge only when the parts interact in a wider whole.

Emergence has been observed in thousands of species and natural structures. Some are so common that we simply take them for granted. Like water. A single water molecule is a very (very) basic molecule, but when a jillion of them are put together, you get cohesion and liquidity; you get a solid form (ice) that expands and floats above its liquid form (water). (Quick reminder: that is contrary to the laws of nature. That is a miracle in front of us every single day that we don't praise God for.)

Atoms become molecules become tissues become organs become organisms. Biology itself (life) is an emergence from chemistry. Biology becomes neurobiology, which emerges into new psychological phenomena. The more complex, the more levels, but it's all integrating levels of emergence.

There are a few basic conditions necessary for emergence to happen.

First, you need very simple rules about how to interact with your neighbour. Emergence works on local rules of attraction and repulsion. Atoms are either attracted or repulsed. The rules for a swarm of starlings for instance (that marvel of synchronicity) may be "stay close to your neighbour" combined with "avoid collision." Each level of emergence is based on just a very few simple rules. Second, you need multiple generations. Not just one generation making these simple choices, but many, many generations. Third, you need randomness. No central organization. No leader. Just thousands and millions of individual choices about the simple rule or rules, made over many generations of the organism. And then, with enough quantity, enough randomness and generations, a new quality emerges.

Maybe the new emergence is an ant colony. Single ants are not smart creatures. Even hundreds of ants together aren't that interesting. But when hundreds of thousands of ants join forces, they do remarkable feats of intelligence, like farming mushrooms and maintaining the temperature of their colony to within a few degrees.

Or another: our brain cells are basically the same neurons as in a fruit fly. But humans have 100,000,000,000 of them, compared to only 100,000 in a fruit fly. Quantity can result in new quality.

GENEROSITY AND THE EMERGENCE OF NEW CREATION

Well, the more I reflect on this scientific phenomenon, the more that I see Yahweh in it all. Remember he said that he is presence that is with us and for us?

Emergence is a lens to understand the constant new creation in an ever-expanding universe. The new creation may be new stars being born, or new babies, or new potatoes. Whatever it is, it is layers upon layers of with-ness and for-ness. Layers upon layers of chemical and biological and psychological choices to participate in a union of presence and a trajectory of support. I am with you and for you. I join you to make whatever new creation will emerge from our working together. A new relationship. A new experience.

This is not a reductive vision of our reality as human beings. It is a big, huge, glorious vision. With this vision, we start to see the Spirit of God, the with-and-for energy of Yahweh, using our daily choices to participate (or not), to literally forge a new creation.

This is what generosity is. Generosity, at its core, is syncing with God's Spirit to join with another in some form of with-ness and for-ness.

- Sure, you can use my lawnmower any time. No point in you buying another one when mine sits in my shed fifteen feet from your lawn.
- Yes, I will bring you casserole when you are sick.

27

- Hey honey, I want to donate more to our church, so that our pastor can be paid enough to raise a family in our city.
- Let's do it! I can give $100,000 to endow a scholarship so that young people can be educated, impacting untold numbers of people throughout their lifetimes.

They are all essentially choices of yes or no. And it is okay to choose either one. (Truly it is. And I will talk about that more below.) If we say yes, something new will be created from this relationship. If we say no, then it won't, and we can simply wait for the next moment of decision.

But here's an important aspect of new emergence/new creation to remember: we don't necessarily know what new thing will be created.

While at Regent, my husband and I came into some money we weren't expecting. We were grateful for the circumstances, but the money was a surprise gift, so we decided to give it away. We sent it to a friend who was trying to earn his PhD in Edinburgh, supporting his young family while studying. I'm so glad we did. At the time, we were poor students too, but that choice to stand "with and for" our friend's dream of a PhD created something new.

Unbeknownst to us, our friend received it at a time of deep discouragement, when he was considering giving up. His experience receiving that gift meant far more than the money that it was. For him, it was a sign from God: if that much money can arrive from Jason and Christie, then God can do anything! God can provide out of nowhere! Out of places one would least expect it. (Don't worry, I didn't take it personally.) He was encouraged to continue, and he finished his PhD. We had hoped the gift would be helpful for him to finish, but we didn't know that it would become for him a symbolic memory for several years to come, to encourage him that God would provide so he could finish his studies.

Every single step of with-ness and for-ness is our chance to participate in some new creation. It is the simple, single choice that we can take or not take. If we do, it will become some new layer of God's kingdom coming, on earth as it is in heaven.

This is true with money, with philanthropy, just the same as it is true with volunteering, with service, with listening, with forgiveness, with prayer. A hundred times a day we are given a choice. A hundred times a day God offers us another dividing path: he's saying, "I could make something new here, something that will be imbued with my character. Do you want to participate?" A hundred times a day, we can join the "with and for" to be a part of God's new creation.

I've been fundraising now for twenty years and I've seen a great variety of ways in which people experience this calling to participate. For some people, they feel their best response is to give to whoever asks. If God puts someone in front of them asking for help, they say yes, even if just to help a little bit. Other people have a clear sense of exactly the cause or group with whom they are called to be "with and for," and they can clearly decline any other invitations to give in order to focus all their giving in their one passion area.

Both are beautiful. Most people are somewhere in between as they sort out their process for philanthropic decision-making. But the abundance of opportunities to participate, whether through philanthropy or through other forms of generosity, means that all of us are regularly choosing. And saying no is a healthy part of the journey.

Whatever the nature of new creation that may occur with any yes, the one thing we can count on is that we will be a part of it. If you join in, you will be part of that deepened relationship, new project, new responsibility, new experience. It is important to honour in this journey that God is also with and for you. Your mental and physical health, your limitations, and your sense of joy or burden are all part of the mixture. What you may or may not become if you say yes or no can be part of your discernment.

The main question to ask is "Holy Spirit, as I incarnate the heart of God to be 'with and for,' to act out solidarity toward some new creation, is this an opportunity I should participate in?"

By its very nature, a yes will create something new. The new thing might be immediate and easy, or it might be forty years in the desert responsible for a grumpy tribe of slaves. You might not see the new creation clearly until you look back decades later.

Whatever you choose to say yes to—to be with and for—bless you. You are incarnating the very heart of God.

3

IT'S ALL GIFT

Psalm 111–112

Richard Thompson

Have you heard the maxim "It's all gift"? Or what about "Yet not I but the grace of God within me"? Both sayings are great because they declare the priority and centrality of God's grace in our lives.

How about this maxim? "Wealth and riches are in their houses, / and their righteousness endures forever" (Psalm 112:3). Pastor Creflo Dollar of World Changers Church International names and claims this verse from Psalm 112 as part of a daily confession that declares God's favour for accumulating wealth.

Another world changer, by the name of Saul of Tarsus, in 2 Corinthians 9:9, also quoted Psalm 112 when writing to his Gentile congregations about the matter of giving and generosity: "They have freely scattered their gifts to the poor; / their righteousness endures forever" (Psalm 112:9).

Both verses are Holy Scripture. Both are found in Psalm 112. Both are true and worthy of our proclamation. But both need to be understood in the context of Psalm 112 and within the wider context of the preceding psalm. And as we shall see, both verses—and both psalms—are rooted deeply in the grace of God. Our wealth and riches are "all gift." And our generous gift giving is "all grace."

Psalm 112 is what is known as a wisdom psalm. The psalmist understands that wisdom begins with the fear of the Lord. The psalm contrasts the righteous person with the wicked person; and it extols the virtues of righteous living, describing the attendant benefits and covenant blessings.

But we need to read and know Psalm 111 before we can read and understand Psalm 112.

THE TWIN PSALMS

Psalms 111 and 112 actually form a unit. They are wonderfully twinned in theme and structure. Together, they form an acrostic. After the opening "Hallelujah" (or "Praise the Lord") in both psalms, each of the 22 lines found in the combined psalms begins with a successive letter of the Hebrew alphabet.

If the two psalms were not written by the same author, then the author of 112 certainly borrowed from 111. There are no less than eleven words or phrases that are identical in the two. And Psalm 112 picks up right where Psalm 111 leaves off: the fear of Yahweh is the beginning of wisdom and all who follow his precepts have good understanding.

So much in theology is based on getting the order right, is it not?

- Creation comes before the Fall—you need that order to get salvation right
- The exodus comes before the law—you need that order to get holiness right
- Psalm 111 comes before Psalm 112—you need that order to get wealth and giving right
- And God's grace and activity comes before everything we do—you need that order to get God right

As Gordon Fee was fond of saying/shouting in our biblical theology course, "The indicative always precedes the *imperative*!" In other words, what God has already done for us in Christ Jesus (the indicative) always precedes any command (the imperative) to do something for the Lord.

Put more simply still: Don't put the cart in front of the horse!

Let's take a closer look at these twin psalms.

Praise the LORD.

I will extol the LORD with all my heart
    in the council of the upright and in the as-
    sembly.

Great are the works of the LORD;
    they are pondered by all who delight in
    them.
Glorious and majestic are his deeds,
    and his righteousness endures forever.
He has caused his wonders to be remembered;
    the LORD is gracious and compassionate.
He provides food for those who fear him;
    he remembers his covenant forever.

He has shown his people the power of his
    works,
    giving them the lands of other nations.
The works of his hands are faithful and just;
    all his precepts are trustworthy.
They are established for ever and ever,
    enacted in faithfulness and uprightness.
He provided redemption for his people;
    he ordained his covenant forever—

holy and awesome is his name.

The fear of the LORD is the beginning of wisdom;
    all who follow his precepts have good under-
    standing.
    To him belongs eternal praise. (Psalm 111)

Praise the LORD.

Blessed are those who fear the LORD,
    who find great delight in his commands.

Their children will be mighty in the land;
    the generation of the upright will be blessed.
Wealth and riches are in their houses,
    and their righteousness endures forever.
Even in darkness light dawns for the upright,
    for those who are gracious and compassion-
    ate and righteous.
Good will come to those who are generous and
    lend freely,
    who conduct their affairs with justice.

Surely the righteous will never be shaken;
    they will be remembered forever.
They will have no fear of bad news;
    their hearts are steadfast, trusting in the
    Lord.
Their hearts are secure, they will have no fear;

in the end they will look in triumph on their
foes.
They have freely scattered their gifts to the poor,
their righteousness endures forever;
their horn will be lifted high in honor.

The wicked will see and be vexed,
they will gnash their teeth and waste away;
the longings of the wicked will come to
nothing. (Psalm 112)

Knowing that the two psalms form a unit allows us to discover the thrust of both. Psalm 111 extols Yahweh for his great works and gracious character as seen in the events of the Exodus and the Mount Sinai covenant, and Psalm 112 extols the human life that is patterned upon the character and activity of Yahweh described in 111.

If we understand that 111 precedes 112, we recognize that Psalm 112 is the outworking of the reality described in Psalm 111. And what is that reality? It's not the wealth of verse 3 that some may claim each morning. No, the central message of the two psalms almost jumps out at us when we notice the wording of verse 4 in each psalm.

111:4b Yahweh is gracious and compassionate

> 112:4b the righteous people of Yahweh are gra-
> cious and compassionate

The latter doesn't happen if the former does not precede it. Our reception of Yahweh's grace and compassion means that we, as his righteous ones, can in turn be people of grace and compassion. You see, the focus of Psalm 112 is *not* the accumulation of wealth by God's people; it is their gracious and compassionate acts, which mirror the righteous character and activity of Yahweh.

Because Psalm 111 is true, Psalm 112 can be true. Because Yahweh provides redemption for the Hebrew slaves in Egypt (111:9), we can scatter abroad our gifts to the poor (112:9). Because Yahweh graciously provides manna and quail for his people in the desert (111:5), we can be generous and lend freely (112:5). Because to Yahweh belongs eternal praise (111:10), our righteous acts will endure forever (112:9).

I remember when my wife and I made the most generous and sacrificial gift of our married lives. We served on the board of a small Christian school—a school that was struggling to pay its bills and payroll. My wife and I felt led to borrow from our line of credit so that we could make a substantial gift to help sustain the school. It wasn't easy. There was no particular experience of being a cheerful, or *hilarious*, giver! We weren't exactly reciting to each other, "It is more blessed to give than to receive." If anything, we were thinking, "It sure hurts more to give than to receive." But there was a sense of having done the right thing, of having been obedient to the Spirit, of being thankful that our children's wonderful teachers would get paid that month. And there was certainly the awareness that our ability to make this gift was due to the abundant grace of God. God's gracious provision was not in the way of an unexpected inheritance or a cash windfall that covered the amount of our donation. His provision was simply the grace and courage to give sacrificially, recognizing that it might be several months before we could pay off our line of credit. Jennifer and I cannot tell the story of our Psalm 112 experience of scattering our gifts to the poor without first telling the Psalm 111 story of God's gracious provision to us.

GOD'S GIVING AND OUR GIVING

Just as Psalm 111 and Psalm 112 need to be read together, so do the stories of God's giving and our giving need to be told together. We shouldn't tell one without the other. When you are tempted to talk about your personal giving, start with the story of God's grace. Likewise, when you're telling the story of God's giving, make sure to tell the exciting sequel of what his grace has enabled you to do!

Do we not see a picture of that in Luke's account of the sinful woman who anointed Jesus with the alabaster jar of expensive perfume?

> When one of the Pharisees invited Jesus to have dinner with him, he went to the Pharisees's house and reclined at the table. A woman in that town who lived a sinful life learned that Jesus was eating at the Pharisee's house, so she came there with an alabaster jar of perfume. As she stood behind him at his feet weeping, she began to wet his feet with her tears. Then she wiped them with her hair, kissed them and poured perfume on them.
>
> When the Pharisee who had invited him saw this, he said to himself, "If this man were a prophet, he would know who is touching him and what kind of woman she is—that she is a sinner."
>
> Jesus answered him, "Simon, I have something to tell you."
>
> "Tell me, teacher," he said.
>
> Two people owed money to a certain moneylender. One owed him five hundred denarii, and the other fifty. Neither of them had the money to pay him back, so he forgave the debts of both. Now which of them will love him more?"
>
> Simon replied, "I suppose the one who had the bigger debt forgiven."

"You have judged correctly," Jesus said.

Then he turned toward the woman and said to Simon, "Do you see this woman? I came into your house. You did not give me any water for my feet, but she wet my feet with her tears and wiped them with her hair. You did not give me a kiss, but this woman, from the time I entered, has not stopped kissing my feet. You did not put oil on my head, but she has poured perfume on my feet. Therefore, I tell you, her many sins have been forgiven—as her great love has shown. But whoever has been forgiven little loves little."

Then Jesus said to her, "Your sins are forgiven."

The other guests began to say among themselves, "Who is this who even forgives sins?"

Jesus said to the woman, "Your faith has saved you; go in peace." (Luke 7:36–50)

When Jesus is challenged by the Pharisee, he tells the parable of the two people who owed debts to a moneylender, and concludes with the powerful indictment, "Whoever has been forgiven little, loves little." When we, like the sinful woman, really get a grasp of just how much we have been forgiven, of how much grace we have received, we will in turn love much and freely pour out our alabaster jars of riches on the Master. *Freely you have received; freely give.*

When the apostle Paul urges the wealthy Corinthians to be generous, using the poor Macedonians as his example of generosity, he quotes Psalm 112:9.

> And God is able to make all grace abound to you, so that in all things, at all times, having all that you need, you will abound in every good work. As it is written: They have scattered abroad their gifts to the poor; their righteousness endures forever. Now he who supplies seed to the sower and bread for food will also supply and increase your store of seed and will enlarge the harvest of your righteousness. You will be made rich in every way so that you can be generous on every occasion, and through us your generosity will result in thanksgiving to God. (2 Corinthians 9:8–11)

Did you notice how Paul got the order right? He writes verse 8 before verse 9! You need that order of God's blessing preceding our generosity if you're going to get the proper understanding of wealth and giving. God supplies all grace so that we have all we need to abound in every good work. God's provision precedes our giving and living. We don't give so that we can get. We get so that we can give! The goal is in the giving; not in the getting. And the difference is absolutely essential.

Lastly, did you also notice how Paul picks up on the two "eternal" threads that run through Psalm 111 and 112? Clearly this man knew his psalter.

In Psalm 111, what endures forever? Yahweh's righteousness and his praise.

In Psalm 112, what endures forever? Our righteous activity of generosity and compassion.

Listen to how Paul links them together at the end of that Corinthian passage: "Your generosity will result in thanksgiving to God." Our righteous acts result in praise to God; our enduring righteousness will be an everlasting expression of praise to the Lord.

Much more could be said about the enduring nature of our righteous acts of generosity and compassion. They have lasting impact. They outlive us and form our legacy. They are recorded and remembered and will be recalled. I've attended my fair share of memorial services over the past couple of years, and I have been struck by the notable legacies of our departed friends. They lived life so well and gave of themselves and of their resources so graciously and freely. While grace remains the motivation and impetus for our giving, the testimonies of these loved ones have been nothing short of inspiring and have caused me to reflect on what will be said of me at my memorial service.

Dear brothers and sisters, it's all gift. Yet not I but the grace of God within me. And remember, 111 comes before 112.

May God grant us the grace to be generous and compassionate, reflecting the character of Yahweh and deflecting all praise and glory back to him.

4

THE UNFORTUNATE CASE OF THE UNCHEERFUL GIVER

Mark 12:41–44

Jeffrey P. Greenman

One of Protestantism's most beloved hymns is Frances Havergal's "Take My Life and Let It Be." It is a classic statement of Christian discipleship. The hymn essentially is a commentary on Romans 12:1, which calls us, "in view of God's mercy, to offer your bodies as a living sacrifice, holy and pleasing to God—this is your true and proper worship." Her hymn is a deeply moving, poetic description of systematic, heartfelt self offering to God. As we sing, worshippers reorient all of our human capacities and resources to God's service. Nothing is held back. Recall how thorough is this offering:

Take my life and let it be consecrated Lord, to
    thee.
Take my moments and my days, let them flow in
    ceaseless praise.
Take my hands and let them move at the impulse
    of thy love.
Take my feet and let them be swift and beautiful
    for thee.

Take my voice and let me sing always, only for
    my king.
Take my lips and let them be filled with messag-
    es from thee.
Take my silver and my gold not a mite would I
    withhold.
Take my intellect and use every power as you
    choose.

The reference to "not a mite would I withhold" is, of course, an allusion to the famous New Testament story of the widow's mite. This verse is sometimes omitted from modern hymnals. Perhaps it is deemed to be too intrusive (or perhaps even objectionable?) to suggest that congregants should withhold none of their silver or gold from the Lord and his service. After all, money is a sensitive topic, one which often we prefer to keep quite private, off limits from the scrutiny of other people, and certainly beyond the scrutiny of the church. Sex, politics, and money are probably the hardest topics to talk about on Sunday mornings. Frequently these are avoided altogether.

CONFRONTING INJUSTICE

When we do talk about money, especially about stewardship, there is one story that is consistently very popular, namely, the account of the widow and her mite, found in Mark 12 (and also in Luke 21). More than any other Bible character, the otherwise anonymous widow is the most likely star of a stewardship sermon.

But you should sense from my title, "The Unfortunate Case of the Uncheerful Giver," that I think we need to rethink the familiar story. If we read the story of her offering in the temple in its biblical context—especially if we read it in light of what comes right before it and right after it—we get a different sense of what's going on, and why the Gospel writers tell us her story.

Let's remember how Mark frames her story within his larger story.

> As he taught, Jesus said, "Watch out for the teachers of the law. They like to walk around in flowing robes and be greeted with respect in the marketplaces, and have the most important

seats in the synagogues and the places of honor
at banquets. They devour widows' houses and for
a show make lengthy prayers. These men will be
punished most severely." (Mark 12:38–40)

At this stage in the story, Jesus is navigating ongo-
ing conflict with the religious leaders around him—
the Pharisees, the Sadducees, and these "scribes."
He's challenging them for their corruption, for their
wrong priorities, for their legalism, and for their fail-
ure to genuinely serve God's people as they should.
He has basically nothing good to say about them, and
he's not going to turn a blind eye to their failures and
mistakes.

Who are these "scribes"? They are leaders within
the Jewish religious establishment. Religiously, their
job was teaching the Torah (or "law") to God's people. Socially, they are the aristocracy; they are highly educated; they are powerful. They are advisors
to the chief priests, so have political power. What's
the problem with them? Jesus is very critical of them
because they "like to walk around in flowing robes,
and be greeted with respect in the marketplaces, and
have the most important seats in the synagogues and
the places of honor at banquets." For Jesus, their behaviour reflects superficial and worldly values—not
the ways of God.

Their behaviour boils down to self-seeking ambition. Being seen and admired is what they care about most. They have a pompous, arrogant attitude. They enjoy having the most important seats, whereby they advance their social standing and keep moving up the social ladder, gaining more power. They like lavish banquets—but the poor in the community go hungry.

With this in mind, verse 40 becomes very important to our story: "They devour widows' houses and for a show make lengthy prayers." What's going on here? We all can understand what showing off with lengthy prayers would look like. Interestingly, the text suggests that their hypocritical piety is trying to cover up some very bad behaviour. Their false piety is a cloak for serious injustice.

What does it mean to "devour widows' houses"? Scholars are not completely agreed about the specific details of the particular injustice they were perpetrating. Clearly this is the economic exploitation of widows, who are the most vulnerable people in the community. The Old Testament is abundantly clear and consistent that religious leaders are to take care of the widows, and orphans, to make sure their needs are met. Instead, we see that the scribes are greedy—they are preying on widows, who are the very people they should be supporting. Some commentators say that they are actually cheating the widows out of their homes by acting as unethical administrators of their estates after their husbands have died. In the process, they are manipulating the widows' inheritances to their own advantage.

Earlier in his ministry, Jesus had also criticized the religious leaders for teaching people that it was their priority to give to the temple even if this giving deprived a person's family of financial support (Mark 7:10-13). This appears to be exactly what's happening to the widow in our story. She is giving to the temple, as was expected for a pious Jew, but her giving is depriving her of what little she has to live on, which is shameful.

The bottom line is simple: the powerful are exploiting and oppressing the vulnerable, resulting in the suffering of widows, and they are wrapping their immorality in a thick layer of showy piety.

A GENEROUS BUT UNFORTUNATE SACRIFICE

This brings us to the episode of their financial giving, about which we read: Jesus sat down opposite the place where the offerings were put and watched the crowd putting their money into the temple treasury. Many rich people threw in large amounts (Mark 12:41).

Jesus observes the situation. He carefully watches the philanthropic action in the temple. There would have been thirteen trumpet-shaped chests, mounted on the walls of the court of women, where people threw in their offerings. The text tells us that many rich people threw in large amounts, but a poor widow came and put in two very small copper coins, worth only a few cents (v. 42). The contrast couldn't be starker. Many rich people versus one poor widow. Huge amounts versus a tiny amount. In fact, the widow's contribution is comically small. She gives all she has: two small copper coins, which were the smallest ones in circulation. They were worth about 1/8 of a cent each—about 1/64 of a day's wages.

Then Jesus interprets the scene. This is a critical learning moment for the disciples. The text says: Calling his disciples to him, Jesus said, "Truly I tell you, this poor widow has put more into the treasury than all the others. They all gave out of their wealth; but she, out of her poverty, put in everything—all she had to live on" (vv. 43-44). The punchline of the entire story is right there: she gave more than all those others.

The idea that she gave more than the wealthy people is what should shock us. And this is the point in the story where we see that the widow's mite is profoundly sad. She's giving all she had to live on. She would go hungry as a result—to be poor in the ancient world was to be hungry. Her giving leaves her destitute, on the fragile borderline of being able to survive. This is a vivid picture of what it looks like for the poor to be exploited by the rich. She is anything but a cheerful giver, which is what the Bible exalts, time and time again. She should be cared for by the temple officials. She should be receiving from them, not giving her last pennies. She is not reported to be a joyful giver. Something seriously wrong has happened here.

Notice carefully what Jesus says and does not say about her. He does not praise her. He does not make her an example to be followed. He doesn't say, "Go and do likewise." He doesn't say, "God must be very pleased with what she did." He does not commend her faith. Why not? I suggest it's because Jesus does not want to endorse a widow ever giving their last pennies to the temple treasury. This should not be happening.

Rather, Jesus makes clear that this sad or even shocking case testifies to the corruption of the temple by its leaders, which deserves God's judgment. He is speaking in condemnation of the pressuring of the poor into giving, even if it means destitution. And Jesus is condemning the kind of the giving that costs us nothing. This echoes the affirmation of King David, who once said "I'm not going to offer God sacrifices that are no sacrifice" (1 Chronicles 21:24 MSG). As a wise preacher commented, "To give without sacrifice is not to give at all."

Put positively, Jesus teaches the disciples, and us, how to morally and spiritually evaluate the contribution she's made. Jesus reframes the question of who is giving more. Jesus has a different way of calculating the significance of donations than we do. In effect, Jesus is saying: "From my perspective, the widow is putting in far more than everyone else. They gave out of their abundance; she gave out of her poverty. In absolute terms, her giving is minuscule. But in proportional terms, her giving is stupendous. She gave exponentially more than the rich people. That totally changes our estimation of whose giving is worth remembering, doesn't it?"

What's happening here is that Jesus is doing what he does so regularly in the Gospels—turning the world's thinking upside down. Here he disrupts and overturns the socially acceptable ways of thinking about money held in his own time and in our contemporary world.

Even today, typically we think that if someone gives big amounts, they must be more important than people who give smaller amounts. It is rather shocking to learn that Jesus is not impressed with the sheer size of someone's donation but by the degree of sacrifice that is involved in their giving. This is worth pondering, as I am aware of a recent study of American philanthropy showing that if you earn less than $12,500 per year, you are likely to give away twice as much on a percentage basis as someone who earns more than $90,000.

Our world is impressed by very large financial gifts—cheques with lots of zeroes on them. Gifts of huge amounts attract a lot of attention. I can testify that sometimes very large gifts are given by godly, humble people with amazing generosity and heartfelt gratitude to God. Such people are not looking for acclaim. However, I can also testify that in some situations very big donations are given to make a show of someone's generosity, to impress others, or to gain praise or stature or importance or power on account of giving a large sum. Sometimes these gifts are given to make an impressive show of one's piety, just as in our story.

CONGREGATIONAL STEWARDSHIP AND PERSONAL GIVING

Where does this story of the widow and her mite leave us? First, let's think about our congregational stewardship.

Having looked carefully at the context of the widow's mite, we should bear in mind that this passage is a cautionary tale. It speaks to the life of every congregation, and to each congregation's stewardship of its resources. The unfortunate case of the uncheerful giver makes clear that the most vulnerable in our society must never be exploited by the church of Jesus Christ. If ever the church pressures or manipulates poor people to give their last pennies to the church, surely that is a mark of injustice rather than faith.

Put positively, our passage reminds each congregation that God's people everywhere and at all times have a special duty to care for widows and orphans, to take care of the needy and most vulnerable by showing them tender-hearted compassion and by extending practical help with the necessities of life. As we read in James 1:27, "Religion that God our Father accepts as pure and faultless is this: to look after orphans and widows in their distress and to keep oneself from being polluted by the world."

Finally, what does this passage suggest for our personal giving?

As you consider your giving to the ministry of your home congregation, or to other Christian charitable causes, if you have been blessed to be able to give a large amount, do not think that fact makes you more important than anyone else or spiritually superior to others who cannot give as much. Do not think that if you give larger gifts, then you are entitled to the best seats in the synagogue or to wield power within the church on account of your financial contribution. Do not use your giving for self-aggrandizement.

If your giving can be a small amount in absolute terms, but a large amount in proportional terms, banish any thought that your donation to God's work is insignificant or unimportant or unnoticed. Do not think that God is more impressed with large amounts than small ones. Do not think you are spiritually inferior if your giving is less than others can give. Jesus' way of evaluating the significance of gifts is not the world's way. Jesus sees and notices every gift, no matter how large or small.

5

THE CONVERSION OF THE WALLET

2 Corinthians 9:1–15

Rod J. K. Wilson

It continues to surprise me that so many people believe that raising money is outside the realm of what it
means to be Christian. With a separation of the material from the spiritual, the human from the transcen-
dent, and money from worship, this lack of integra-
tion shows up both in a secular perspective that does
not see faith as integral to all of life and in a sacred
framework where trusting God is seen as antithetical
to requesting funds.

For those who believe that fundraising is a "dirty
business," lacking in virtue and nobility, chapters 8–9
of 2 Corinthians are arresting. Following chapters
1–7, which are biographical in nature and provide a

defense of Paul's apostolic ministry and his experience with hardships, and preceding chapters 10–13, which focus on Paul's strength in weakness as support for his apostolic authority, chapters 8–9 provide a detailed analysis of fundraising.

Based on the financial need of the Jewish believers in Jerusalem and the example of the Macedonian Christians who gave generously, Paul solicits funds from the Corinthians with a direct and overt appeal. In fact, one could easily argue that 2 Corinthians 8 is one of the most aggressive fundraising appeals in the Bible. As he moves into chapter 9, he makes one more specific overture for the local need and then articulates general principles and practices for giving. It is to those details that we now turn our attention.

CONTEXT (9:1–5)

There is no need for me to write to you about this service to the Lord's people. For I know your eagerness to help, and I have been boasting about it to the Macedonians, telling them that since last year you in Achaia were ready to give; and your enthusiasm has stirred most of them to action. But I am sending the brothers in order that our boasting about you in this matter should not prove hollow, but that you may be ready, as I said you would be. For if any Macedonians come with me and find you unprepared, we—not to say anything about you—would be ashamed of having been so confident. So I thought it necessary to urge the brothers to visit you in advance and finish the arrangements for the generous gift you had promised. Then it will be ready as a generous gift, not as one grudgingly given.

There is a tongue-in-cheek feel to the first verse in this chapter. If there is no need to write about it, why has he already devoted an entire chapter to the matter and is now revisiting it again?! But Paul believes he must remind them that they have promised but have not delivered. They professed an eagerness to give in the past, and he actually used that to motivate the Macedonians. While "compare and contrast" may not be seen as an appropriate fundraising tactic for Christian fundraisers, the apostle appears to have no reticence. It's as if he's saying: "I told those other people you promised money, so they have taken your cue and have given enthusiastically. What is your problem?"

As the appeal continues you get a clear sense that Paul is not impressed with the church at Corinth. He fears their promise is hollow, they are not ready to give, and not even prepared. A lack of delivery on the pledge may create eventual shame, which would not only be shared by Paul and the Macedonians but quite likely by the Corinthians too. And this is personal for Paul, as his boasting about the church was based on confidence that they would come through. The reality that they seem to be over-promising and under-delivering leads him to wonder whether they are committed to generosity or mired in a grudging spirit. Paul's tolerance of talk without action is not high.

PRINCIPLE (9:6)

> Remember this: Whoever sows sparingly will also reap sparingly, and whoever sows generously will also reap generously.

It is not insignificant that the Corinthians' lack of pledge completion led the apostle to use their misstep to lay out the ideal path. While he tried the compare and contrast mode, with the infusion of persuasion and shame, he now positions giving in a larger context by outlining an important principle.

We once had a neighbour who had a lovely garden every April. Tulips were vibrant and perfectly located throughout the property. Colour combinations were ideal and leafy bushes framed various collections in beautiful ways. I often stood in my garden envious of my neighbour's grand display (an instance of coveting not specifically mentioned in the Tenth Commandment) irritated at the rather pathetic array of plants in our yard.

Envy makes no sense in this context because the difference between our gardens was not measured best in April but in the previous year. He had done the work. I had not. It is exactly this image that Paul is capturing when it comes to money. Those of us who are stingy and cling to our money do not see the priority of sowing seed in a generous way. A sparse outcome is inevitable. Significant kingdom impact and influence, on the other hand, is a natural by-product of those who plant generously.

It is really the "if-then" of wisdom. Foolish people do not connect behaviour and consequences, believing that what one does is unrelated to the outcome of what one does. Wise people, in contrast, understand that while there is not always a perfect guarantee, sowing righteousness through the use of our money will produce a rich harvest.

PRACTICE (9:7)

> Each of you should give what you have decided in your heart to give, not reluctantly or under compulsion, for God loves a cheerful giver.

One of the things I love about Scripture is that it not only provides the theological foundation for why we need to engage in particular behaviours, but it also offers practical steps in how to make that happen. Here in one simple verse, the apostle offers three windows into how we should give.

Participation. There is no focus in this passage on our age, income, employment, how well we are paid, our monthly expenses, or whether we bring an abundance or scarcity mindset to the table. It is assumed that we all give. There is something leveling about this approach. Once we understand the biblical context and the reaping-sowing principle, giving is inevitable.

Decision. In an age of skills, gimmicks, and techniques, where we are bombarded by requests for money, the simplicity of this passage cries out. It is a decision of the heart. Consciously, thoughtfully, and prayerfully we determine what we need to give. Such a posture presupposes communion with God, a sensitivity to the needs around us, and a volitional engagement that considers our own finances. In the first epistle to Corinth, Paul indicated that this choice should be made "in keeping with your income" (1 Corinthians 16:2).

Motivation. While we can participate in giving and be intentional in doing so, we need to answer the why question. Why do we give? What drives it? What is our motivation? Again, the specificity of the biblical material is noteworthy. Paul talks about internal and external dynamics when it comes to motivation. Our inner life should not be characterized by reluctance— or literally "out of sorrow"—but with a liberality without a holding back. By the same token, the external forces in our lives should not create compulsion or arm twisting.

Too much of the charity world misunderstands this variable and believes that strong and aggressive requests for money will result in more gifts. Rather we should be attentive to and striving for hilarious or cheerful giving. Godly givers understand the difference between laughing all the way *to* the bank and laughing all the way *from* the bank.

FOUNDATION (9:8–11A)

And God is able to bless you abundantly, so that in all things at all times, having all that you need, you will abound in every good work. As it is written:

"They have freely scattered their gifts to the poor; their righteousness endures forever."

Now he who supplies seed to the sower and bread for food will also supply and increase your store of seed and will enlarge the harvest of your righteousness. You will be enriched in every way so that you can be generous on every occasion.

Sometimes when we present an argument for why something is important, we commence with the foundational premise, laying out the theory and structure and then move into what to do. Based on an older notion, that practice always follows theory, we forget that there is often a reciprocal relationship between the two. Engaging in behaviour sometimes forces you back to what undergirds your actions. Such is the case in this chapter.

When confronted with the responsibility to give money, it is easy to bring a scarcity mindset. Where is the money coming from? How will I survive? As if to anticipate such an objection, Paul reminds us that the source of our money is God himself. It is he who blesses, and because of that we can have an abundance mindset. In all things. At all times. Having all that we need. We will abound in every good work. A posture of contentment with what we have is the platform for giving.

In a culture where we conceptualize ourselves as working for money, it is quite a challenge to see God lurking behind our salary. And an even greater challenge to see His financial blessing as not an opportunity to hoard, collect, and consume but rather to give. Using the language of Psalm 112, Paul sees the distribution of our financial gifts to the poor producing righteousness that has eternal impact.

Second Corinthians 9:10–11 describes a giving cycle that pulls it all together. The focus is not on isolated acts of giving but on a lifestyle of stewardship where God, the giver, and the receiver are in right perspective. God, as the giver of every good and perfect gift, provides us with financial resources, which come from grace and produce gratitude. That gratitude in turn becomes an impetus for giving. In contrast to consuming and craving, both of which lead to keeping, others benefit from our giving because we are stimulated by grace and live it out in gratitude. But this is a cyclical process. God continues to provide us with more seed, so we can do more sowing, with the outcome of a larger harvest.

Abuses of this principle do show up in kingdom work. Individuals and churches, adhering to a so-called "prosperity gospel," work on the assumption that more giving will result in more being given to you. This is an accurate reading of the text in its context. However, if the "more" is simply for our benefit, increased financial security, or accumulation of more goods, then we have departed from what this passage teaches. The more is not for the benefit of self but for the benefit of the other.

CONSEQUENCES (9:11B-14)

> And through us your generosity will result in
> thanksgiving to God. This service that you per-
> form is not only supplying the needs of the Lord's
> people but is also overflowing in many expres-
> sions of thanks to God. Because of the service by
> which you have proved yourselves, others will
> praise God for the obedience that accompanies
> your confession of the gospel of Christ, and for
> your generosity in sharing with them and with
> everyone else. And in their prayers for you their
> hearts will go out to you, because of the surpass-
> ing grace God has given you.

Contemporary philanthropy focuses on what your
money will buy. Give to this project and a new build-
ing will be put up. Donate to this cause and hungry
people will be fed. Needs will be met. Desires will be
fulfilled. While this has its place and is an important
component of the giving and receiving of money, Paul
seems to touch on it lightly. Your gifts, he argues, will
meet the needs of the Lord's people, but what is most
important to him is that it will be linked with worship
and prayer.

Such an economy turns what we normally see on
its head. Money given for particular needs runs the
risk of being a sales transaction. We have a product.
We are going to market it diligently. If you succumb,

you will be the answer to our problem, the solution to our challenge. But if we understand God as the source of the seed, then all philanthropy has grace at its core, giving as its expression, and gratitude as its outcome. Providing money becomes a form of worship to God, as does the reception of the money.

Not surprisingly this whole section is filled with various manifestations of thankfulness and relational connectedness, with God at the centre. Nowhere in either chapter 8 or 9 do we read of the nature of the need that the Jewish believers experienced. This is quite a paradox when you think about it. An in-depth elucidation of fundraising makes no mention of what the money will be raised for—a point that may well suggest that there is a lot more going on in the world of philanthropy than transactional payment for compelling projects.

CONCLUSION (9:15)

> Thanks be to God for his indescribable gift!

It is noteworthy that the Greek word *charis* is used ten times in these two chapters. Normally translated in English as "grace" or "gift," it is used by Paul in various ways as it pertains to the giving and receiving of money. One wonders whether Paul was reflecting on this word as he wrote and, typical of his style, moved out of teaching into doxology. How could he talk about how grace, gift, and gratitude envelop the philanthropic space without being thankful for the greatest gift of all, the Lord Jesus Christ? God is more than the source of the seed, which is our money; he is the provider of the ultimate, indescribable gift. Stunning that a heartfelt worship statement concludes two chapters on fundraising!

Although there is debate as to its veracity, it has been reported over the years that Martin Luther claimed that when someone comes to Christ there are three conversions: a conversion of the mind, a conversion of the heart, and a conversion of the wallet. Most of us have an intuitive and experiential understanding of the first two. We know that the transformation of the mind and a renewal of the entire inner person are crucial components of the life that has experienced conversion. With a careful understanding of 2 Corinthians chapter 8, and particularly chapter 9, we may get a small glimpse of what a conversion of the wallet really looks like.

6

FROM MONEY TO DOXOLOGY

Philippians 4:10–20

Nicole Den Haan

We begin with a prayerful presentation of a beautiful passage from the apostle Paul, drawn from the chapter we will be exploring in this sermon. It is a rendering of Philippians 4:4-9 in the form of a corporate call to worship.

> Gracious Triune God,
> > as we gather today, may we rejoice in you;
> > **may we rejoice in you always.**
> As we remind ourselves that you are near,
> > **help us cast aside all anxiety.**
> As we remind ourselves that you are near,

give us thankful hearts as we present our requests to you.
As we remind ourselves that you are near,
send your peace, which transcends all understanding,
to guard our hearts and minds.
Brothers and sisters in Christ,
as we contemplate truth and goodness,
the God of peace is with us.
As we think on things that are excellent and
praiseworthy,
the God of peace is with us.
As we put into practice what we have received
from God,
the God of peace is with us.
The Lord is near; we give him praise.[1]

"MONEY" IN CHRIST

While in a written text we don't have the benefit of
moving from a call to worship to singing together
about the goodness of the Lord in hymns like "Praise
to the Lord, the Almighty" and "Joyful, Joyful, We
Adore You," it is with this posture of praise that we
should approach the question rising from Philippians

1. Arranged by Corey Janz, Regent College Worship Co-
ordinator.

4:10–20. How does Paul move from money to doxology to praise?

> I rejoiced greatly in the Lord that at last you renewed your concern for me. Indeed, you were concerned, but you had no opportunity to show it. I am not saying this because I am in need, for I have learned to be content whatever the circumstances. I know what it is to be in need, and I know what it is to have plenty. I have learned the secret of being content in any and every situation, whether well fed or hungry, whether living in plenty or in want. I can do all this through him who gives me strength.
>
> Yet it was good of you to share in my troubles. Moreover, as you Philippians know, in the early days of your acquaintance with the gospel, when I set out from Macedonia, not one church shared with me in the matter of giving and receiving, except you only; for even when I was in Thessalonica, you sent me aid more than once when I was in need. Not that I desire your gifts; what I desire is that more be credited to your account. I have received full payment and have more than enough. I am amply supplied, now that I have received from Epaphroditus the gifts you sent. They are a fragrant offering, an acceptable sacrifice, pleasing to God. And my God will meet all your needs according to the riches of his glory in Christ Jesus.

To our God and Father be glory for ever and
ever. Amen.

The answer may seem obvious to those of us who
have grown up in Christian contexts: all that we have,
including our money, comes from God, and we are to
return it to God in praise and thanksgiving. If that's
the case, though, why is money commonly an un-
pleasant thing to talk about even for those of us who
count ourselves as brothers and sisters in Christ? It's
complicated, to be sure. Yet, we see in Paul's letter to
the Philippians that he lives his life so thoroughly in
Christ that he sees the work of God even in the seem-
ingly mundane and distasteful.

As someone who has found herself working in a
field that uses unclear titles like "advancement" or
"development," when I explain what I do—fundraising—they look at me with some combination of con-
fusion, bafflement, and sometimes even awe, based
on, I think, all kinds of assumptions about money. Far
from pushy salesperson techniques, the kind of fundraising I do, given its Regent College context, means
listening to our donors' stories and hearing where the
Spirit is moving in places and lives with whom I'd
otherwise have little contact. I tell Regent's stories
of suffering and joy and about what I and others see
God doing in and through Regent's students, staff,

faculty, grads, and donors. I have the privilege of sitting across from people who support this place with their finances and their care. It is because I know our donors that when I see a donation come in, I struggle to find appropriate words of gratitude. "Thank you" is a great place to start, but it just doesn't seem to do the job justice. What am I thanking *for*? For someone giving to Regent? Yes, but is that it? What are they giving *to*? Are they giving to Regent? Yes, but is that it?

By the power of the Holy Spirit, Regent College "cultivates intelligent, vigorous, and joyful commitment to Jesus Christ, His church, and His world." This is what Regent's donors give to. These brothers and sisters in Christ live in normal houses and fancy houses; they drive normal cars and fancy cars. They have received provision and they have suffered loss. They are giving to Regent what they could have kept for themselves because they believe that the hope of the gospel is somehow growing through this place and people.

Here's the piece that blows me away every time I sit down with someone over coffee or (so much!) tea: that *their* giving makes *us* recipients. We are in partnership with them, in Christ, to the glory of God. They are in our work here, whether it's the work of a student, faculty member, staff person, or even the extended work of our graduates and lifelong learning friends. More truly, it is their work, too, even if they live many kilometres away, because it is the work of God in which they're participating.

With these things in mind, "Thank you" seems too feeble a response to someone's willing and sacrificial gift to and participation in God's redemption through Regent College. This is what Paul does, though. He thanks the Philippians for their partnership in the gospel and—may I say this?—it's a bit awkward.

Allow me to paraphrase the beginning of Philippians 4, where the above call to worship came from. Paul has just delivered his final exhortation: "Rejoice! Do not be anxious. Present your requests to God. And the peace of God will guard you. Think about good things. Put into practice what you've learned from me. And the God of peace will be with you."

And then a switch: "I rejoiced greatly in the Lord that you renewed your concern for me. I mean, you were concerned but you didn't have a chance to show it. I'm not thankful because I needed it, per say, since I have learned contentment in all circumstances, whether in need or in plenty. I do this through him who gives me strength. At the same time, I appreciate that you shared in my troubles. Not that I look for your gift since what I want is for you to receive a re-ward at the day of Christ. That said, I do have enough now that you've sent your gifts. And, God will provide for your every need. To him be glory for ever."

It's a bit dizzying, isn't it? As I repeatedly read this text, I felt like I was being pulled in multiple directions at once: *Thank you, but I didn't need it, because I've learned contentment in Christ, but I do have enough now thanks to you. God will provide for you. To God be the glory.*

I know this "back and forthness" that Paul exhibits, the seeming awkwardness of putting into words the partnership that we have with each other in Christ, especially when it involves provision that ultimately is from God *and* has come from the hand of another. That said, I'm not like Paul: I haven't learned the secret of being content in all circumstances. I would rather have more than less, to feel financially and materially secure in ways that I can control. Maybe we all, if we're honest, feel the same. Many of us have been trained through our society's practices and messages to desire and trust money as the means of meeting all our needs.

In Philippians 4, Paul disarms money, but not by ignoring it and thereby allowing it to function by itself, gaining power and dictating the systems of its own world. He disarms it by refusing to allow it to operate its own world. Money doesn't have autonomous power when seen as it truly is in the light of

God's abundance and provision. It doesn't have the power to pit us against each other in light of the unity of our life in Christ. To set the context for a discussion on how money, and specifically a monetary gift, finds its place in a life of doxology, let's look at three examples of unity in Christ in the text.

THE UNITING POWER OF CHRIST

First, locating the Philippians. Paul plunges into his letter by locating himself as a servant of Christ Jesus and themselves as God's holy people in Christ Jesus at Philippi. Being "in Christ" is what Lynn Cohick calls Paul's shorthand for everything stemming from "the actions of God the Father and Christ the Son in our redemption and new life."[2] She is thinking of the incarnation, death, resurrection, exaltation, and return of Christ. Layered into this are various prepositions like "with, through, by, into, and in" which describe the many ways we can see our relationship to Christ as Paul saw the Philippians' relationship to Christ.

These are God's holy people in Christ. They are also at Philippi and Paul is writing to them from his suffering into theirs. This is ground-stomping, "feel-

2. Lynn H. Cohick, *Philippians*, The Story of God Bible Commentary Series, ed. Tremper Longman III and Scott McKnight (Grand Rapids: Zondervan, 2013), 13.

the-world-around-you" reality. These people living in the Roman province of Macedonia likely suffered economic difficulties like job loss as well as familial brokenness because they confessed Christ as Lord. Being in Christ did not spare them from circumstantial suffering.

Moving to the second instance of living in the unity of Christ, you've probably heard Philippians 4:6–7: "Do not be anxious about anything, but in everything, by prayer and petition, present your requests to God." It follows from the previous verse where we see how we can actually live that way: "The Lord is near." Into the Philippians' suffering Paul writes that the Lord is near now and in his return. If you've been around Regent College even a little, you may find the phrase "already but not yet" growing deeply within you, helping you to live in the tensions of life's joy and suffering. It is that phrase that describes the current presence of God's kingdom on earth by the Spirit and the future coming of his kingdom in fullness. Paul emphasizes the current reality of the Lord's nearness in Philippians 1:19, writing that the help given by the Spirit of Christ will turn his suffering into deliverance. That help is given now.

Jesus is also near in his return. In Philippians 1:4 Paul is joyful when he prays for the Philippians because he knows that God will complete his work in them until the day of Christ Jesus. He counts himself *with* them, writing in 3:20–21 that "our citizenship is in heaven and we eagerly await a Saviour from there who, by the power that enables him to bring everything under his control, will transform our lowly bodies so that they will be like his glorious body." This is the "not yet" that Paul encouraged the Philippians to hope for and that we too cling to as we face daily life.

Third, the language that Paul uses in his letter is emotive, not purely intellectual. Even just above we see him exhorting the Philippians to "eagerly await." Paul isn't just reporting facts addressed to their minds. He is writing to them with affection that he ties to Christ's affection, our third instance of unity in Christ. In 1:8 he shares that he is longing for them with the affection of Christ Jesus. Philippians 1:25 reads, "I know that I will continue with all of you for your progress and joy in the faith, so that through *my* being with *you* again *your* joy *in Christ Jesus* will overflow on account of *me*." Gordon Fee calls this a "three way bond," setting Paul's use of "partnership" apart from the normal "one to one."[3] We can pic-

3. Gordon D. Fee, *Paul's Letter to the Philippians*, New International Commentary on the New Testament (Grand Rapids: Eerdmans, 1995), 444.

ture a triangle with Paul, the Philippians, and Christ, where love is flowing through each party.

These three examples—being in Christ and at Philippi, the Lord's present and coming nearness, and Paul's affection as God's affection—show us that partnership in the gospel is more than an earthbound, hand-shaking relationship. It *is* that *and* it's something else too. Turning back to Philippians 4, let's look at giving as one instance where this lands in particularity. That is, the occasion of a monetary gift, which is one way that the generosity of our faith expresses itself.

MONEY AND MORE

In Philippians 4:10–20—and here I'm borrowing from Lynn Cohick—Paul uses commercial language. The Greek verb he uses for "to share" in 4:14 can carry financial overtones; the term *credited* can also mean "profit" or "return." Paul uses more financial, transactional language when he writes of "full payment." But, in all this, here's the key for us: "This vocabulary is interwoven with liturgical language of sacrifice, shaping what could sound utilitarian into a celebration of faithful giving that enriches the community."[4]

4. Cohick, *Philippians*, 249.

If we hear Paul well, we might hear something that is bigger than meeting needs and responding to demands. Perhaps you've had glimpses or experiences of this, where God lifts your head and opens your eyes to *see* what is actually happening, to cause something in your heart – not in the flimsy sense but the robust sense—in your gut, really—to actually draw you into something beyond yourself, beyond where you're giving, and into Christ himself as he works to redeem all things. As Paul understands, the Philippians' gift is a sign to him of their sanctification, their progress in the gospel. Gordon Fee, commenting on this passage writes, "What counts is what God is doing in their lives."[5] What God is doing is evidenced as they live the gospel in their suffering bodies through their willingness to unclench and to offer.

It is good to give. It is good to be grateful, to say thank you. But, as I read Paul, I see a reality through his eyes that both includes and goes beyond the acts of giving and gratitude. Paul neither ignores nor discounts their gift; he sees it truly as part of a much grander reality. As Paul explains, it is you and me doing the giving—he thanks actual people in an actual place—*and* it is God who meets all of our needs, whether we are the giver or receiver.

5. Fee, *Philippians*, 447.

In the Greco-Roman world this kind of partnership involving money could result in one-upping. If you didn't do better than the gift you received, you'd come under a long-term obligation, allowing one party the upper hand.[6] Not so here. Because it's not about the money, actually. It's about being in Christ, who is sufficient for us and who levels the potential hierarchical patron-client relationship to one of mutual belonging. Paul's confidence in Christ's sufficiency allows him to join in doxology with the Philippians, saying, "Look what God has done in and through and for us!"

The trajectory of Paul's thinking is multidimensional in the best way. He starts with Christ. He notes the moment—the gift—and is grateful for it in a tangible way. He demonstrates how it is sign and expression of how he and the Philippians are in Christ together. He explains that he has learned to be content in need—which was probably more common for him—and in bounty. He explains that he didn't *need* their giving because of Christ's strength in him for all circumstances. In the same way, even though they gave out of their own situation of suffering, God will meet all of *their* needs according to his glorious riches in Christ Jesus. And together with the Philippians, in

6. Fee, *Philippians*, 444.

what Fee calls a "final outburst of praise," he gives thanks and praise to our God and Father.[7]

How could we get from *money* to doxology? "True theology is doxology, and doxology is always the proper response to God, even—especially?—in response to God's prompting friends to minister to friends."[8]

For Paul, it's easy. He doesn't actually go anywhere in terms of a movement from a supposed "base reality" involving transaction and funds to a higher ground of praise. He "simply" sees things as they are held together *in Christ*.

How might I respond, then, to donors? In the same way that I hope to respond to all the gifts of life: "Thank you, and *praise God*!" We are all recipients of his wide and unique graces that come to us in the context and form of "ground stomping reality." Paul's view of being in Christ is where we start and end. It's where we are and where we find each other, brothers and sisters, as we look around. His view, this view, is what causes doxology.

May God give us eyes to see ourselves and each other as living in and under the sufficiency of Christ who holds all things—all the separate worlds that we

7. Fee, *Philippians*, 449.
8. Fee, *Philippians*, 455.

create and allow to cloud our thinking, fragment our lives, and sever the unity of our vision of life, whether it is our families, our things, our careers, our time, our work, our rest, our friends, our church, our heads and hearts, our politics, our money. Christ holds all these together. And, as receivers and partakers of his life, he holds us together.

7

ALWAYS, EVERYTHING, AND WHATEVER

*1 Thessalonians 5:16–18, Philippians 4:4–7,
Colossians 3:15–17*

Stephen W. T. Stinton

I love Thanksgiving.[1] Having grown up in the United States, the Canadian version still feels a bit too early. Truth be told, I have actually celebrated Thanksgiving six times in the past three years, since moving to

---

1. I want to acknowledge that there are serious unacknowledged (let alone unresolved) problems and injustice surrounding the history and national myth story of American Thanksgiving. I am genuinely glad that Canada has begun to formally acknowledge our national foundational injustice, and I pray that the United States eventually will too.

Vancouver. One of the major perks of being an American/Canadian transplant is the excuse to celebrate Thanksgiving twice a year. In fact, double celebration seems quite fitting, given that the American holiday is typically marked by over-indulgence.

Beyond the traditional meal and family time, I genuinely like this civil holiday because I personally need a reminder to be thankful. I am not naturally thankful, and so it seems healthy to pause, reflect, and express thanksgiving. In fact, it seems biblical too.

But then I come to a text like 1 Thessalonians 5:16–18, and my comfort is shaken a bit. *Always* celebrate. *Never* stop praying. Give thanks *in every circumstance*. Or as Eugene Peterson translates it in *The Message*: Thank God *no matter what happens*. "No matter what happens"? Surely Paul can't mean that, right?

Of course, having received training at Regent, I confronted this question by immediately dissecting the Greek grammar. In this instance, not much is lost in translation. Sure, it is important to observe that Paul exhorts us to be thankful "in" every circumstance, and *not* "for" every circumstance. But he really does say: "Always rejoice. Never strop praying. Give thanks in every circumstance." And sure, he is addressing a corporate worship setting, but that does not preclude personal application.

Personally, I like an *annual* (or *bi-annual*) holiday. I like a *rhythm* of pausing, reflecting, and thanking—especially during difficult seasons of life. I like seasons of rejoicing and seasons of not-rejoicing (such as mourning), seasons of giving thanks and seasons of . . . not giving thanks?

But Paul did not have a holiday. He had a lifestyle. Or maybe it is better to say that God has a lifestyle that he wills for us. "Rejoice always, pray continually, give thanks in everything; for this is God's will for you in Christ Jesus" (1 Thessalonians 5:16–18).

Rejoicing, praying, and giving thanks are certainly easy during the high points of life. In May 2019, I finally finished my master of arts in theological studies (MATS) degree. It was a difficult and grueling endeavor, so celebration and thanksgiving were in order. And there was much rejoicing.

A few weeks before that, my wife and I both received great job offers during the same week. Again, celebration and thanksgiving were in order. God answered our prayers. God has been very good to us.

But almost exactly one year prior, my wife and I experienced the joy of discovering an unexpected (and life-disrupting) pregnancy, soon followed by the agony of discovering that it was not viable after all. Miscarriage really is as painful as people say. We spent much time crying out to God—literally crying, with tears—but the miscarriage still happened. In fact, we had to wait several weeks for it to actually happen, living in morbid anticipation until it did.

Always rejoice? Pray continually? Thank God in every circumstance?

Last summer, we drove back to Vancouver from a family reunion in the Okanagan—a routine drive that I have done several times. But this time, I apparently developed a blood clot on the way. The clot was superficial—not the more serious deep vein thrombosis—and after a few weeks, it resolved. But when I followed up with a specialist, this doctor had no idea what may have caused it. And I was decades younger than every other patient in that office. Just months later, right before Christmas, I developed another superficial clot in my other leg. At this moment as I write, I am halfway through another round of blood thinners, and the clot seems to have resolved. Yet mystery still surrounds the cause of these clots.

Always rejoice? Pray continually? Thank God in every circumstance?

I am sure you can understand how my cynicism can sneak out when I read a text like this. When I think deeply about what Paul is exhorting us to, it is difficult for me not to think of *Candide*, the satire by Voltaire, which lampooned the simplistic idea that this is "the best of all possible worlds". It feels like there is a naïve optimism that does not align with the realities we often live in.

Of course, it is important to recognize that Paul is *not* saying that type of thing here! Paul is certainly *not* saying that everything that happens in our lives is for the best, but he is saying to give thanks within every circumstance.

As I was meditating on 1 Thessalonians 5, it struck me how similar this text is to Philippians 4:4–6:

> Rejoice in the Lord always. I will say it again: Rejoice! . . . Do not be anxious about anything, but in every situation, by prayer and petition, with thanksgiving, present your requests to God.

And then there's Colossians 3:15–17, where Paul subtly weaves being thankful into his broad ethical commands to love one another and to submit to Christ's lordship.

> Let the peace of Christ rule in your hearts, since as members of one body you were called to peace. And be thankful. Let the message of Christ dwell among you richly as you teach and admonish one another with all wisdom through psalms, hymns, and songs from the Spirit, singing to God with gratitude in your hearts. And whatever you do, whether in word or deed, do it all in the name of

the Lord Jesus, giving thanks to God the Father through him.

Paul remarkably concludes this section by underscoring that whatever we do, in word or deed, we should do in the name of Jesus, giving thanks to the Father.

If you have been "keeping score" to this point, we are told to rejoice *always*, and to be thankful *in everything* (every circumstance), and to give thanks in *whatever* we say or do.

Rejoicing and being thankful permeate these texts. And yet their life setting is strikingly different than that of 1 Thessalonians.

First Thessalonians, arguably Paul's first letter, was probably written in AD 50 or 51, when Paul was still free and planting churches. He had been run out of Thessalonica shortly after proclaiming the gospel, and he had just heard a report from Timothy that a church indeed took root. In fact, this church was thriving! Paul had much to celebrate, and he had the freedom to do so.

Philippians was likely written five to ten years later. Paul was in prison, awaiting a trial that could result in his execution. He was writing to his close friends in the Philippian church, who had just delivered a gift to him.

Colossians was likely written around AD 60–62, while Paul was again in prison. As far as we know, Paul did not plant this church, and he may not have ever even visited it. He seems to have known Epaphras, but he may or may not have known anyone else there.

Strikingly, Paul gives very similar exhortations to these different churches at different stages of his ministry. His message did not change. *Always rejoice in the Lord. Never stop praying. In everything give thanks.*

He wrote this to churches he planted and to those he did not. He wrote it to long-time friends, to believers he had just recently met, and to other Christians he may not have met yet. He said it in the "prime" of his active ministry career and while he was in prison facing execution.

In fact, a lot happened during that decade between 1 Thessalonians, Philippians, and Colossians. Paul was

- beaten with a rod three times
- shipwrecked three times
- spent a night and a day adrift in open sea
- received a whipping of thirty-nine lashes— five times!
- stoned

And these are just a few examples that we know about (2 Corinthians 11:24-33).

Paul faced all sorts of other dangers, and yet perhaps the most discouraging was that, from all accounts, the majority of those who heard Paul's gospel rejected it. Imagine: Paul was commissioned with the task of proclaiming the crucified and resurrected Messiah and the now disclosed mystery of the Jew + Gentile church infused with the Spirit. He received this commissioning in dramatic fashion from the resurrected Lord Jesus himself. And over the course of ten to twenty years, far more people rejected his message than accepted it.

If anyone had reason to be discouraged, or to feel like his faith was being deconstructed, it was Paul.

And yet he wasn't.

Paul is consistently thankful. He is consistently joyful. He is always celebrating. In fact, you see this in his letters. It is no coincidence that he thanks God for the recipients almost every time. He celebrates being in prison, because the gospel is being proclaimed to new people because of it. He celebrates receiving the Philippians' gift because of what it represents with respect to the Philippians' relationship with God.

For Paul, being thankful was not a matter of etiquette or social mores; it was a mode of worship. To give thanks is to acknowledge my dependence on the

Creator and Sustainer of life. It is to recognize that God is in control and to place God in the center of my universe. Doing that, in turn, displaces my own position at the center of the universe.

In fact, in Romans 1 Paul intriguingly points out two characteristics of idolaters: they neither glorify God nor give thanks to him. Why? Failing to thank God is to fail to recognize who he is as the Creator and Sustainer of life.

Thus, thanksgiving is not merely a response to receiving a gift but a core conviction and orientation of one's entire being. It is a worshipful posture recognizing who God is and expressing thanks in response to his character.

I like having seasons of conscious thankfulness and seasons of not thinking about it. But Paul exhorts us to live is a posture toward our Creator that results in us giving thanks to him in the name of Jesus. Always, in everything, and in whatever we say or do.

When my wife and I both received job offers on consecutive days, our expression of gratitude acknowledged and reminded us that they came from God. We did not earn or create these opportunities ourselves.

And when receiving news about a miscarriage, expressing gratitude acknowledged and reminded us that God is still good, that he is present, and that he is in control. Even if we don't understand the "why" of our current circumstances.

In fact, when I thought back to some of the recent difficult times that I have shared here, I distinctly remembered how I prayed because it was so surprising.

I remember when my wife and I were first told that it appeared that this pregnancy would end in a miscarriage. I remember crying and not knowing what to pray. I opened my mouth to see what would happen (seriously), and the first words out of my mouth were "thank you." Father, Thank you that you are the giver of life. Thank you that are here with us. Thank you that you know our pain and agony. Thank you that we can bring this to you in prayer. Thank you that we even have access to you like this, and thank you that we can endure this terrible situation in the midst of your presence.

Something strangely similar happened when we got home from the hospital last August after the doctors determined that I had a blood clot (after five consecutive days in the emergency room!). Again, the first words out of my mouth were "thank you." Thank you that the doctors figured this out. Thank you that they know what it is and how to treat it. Thank you that you are my ultimate healer. Thank you that I have access to an emergency room. Thank you that I didn't bring home a hospital bill.

Honestly, I remember when I started praying about the miscarriage, I was genuinely surprised at the words that were coming out of my mouth. These words were not what I was thinking in my mind. And I am still surprised even writing this now because I am not naturally thankful, and I am not that "spiritual." Honestly, this can only be the Spirit's work.

As I have reflected upon this further, I have realized that I actually do not know how to pray without starting with "thank you." It feels weird when I do not begin a prayer with thanking God for something. But where did I learn this habit?

To be honest, I cannot remember precisely. But I do recall a particular Thanksgiving sermon I heard within the past six or seven years. I recall being challenged to include thanksgiving whenever I prayed for the next thirty days. So for a month, I made an intentional effort to thank God for something every time I prayed. After forgetting a few times, I recall deciding to always do this at the beginning, just so I would not forget.

Yes, at first it was forced. I struggled with sarcasm and cynicism. When we start new routines, awkwardness and difficulty are inevitable. But I pressed on and persevered.

Eventually, this habit stuck. Or rather, the Holy Spirit caused it to stick. And I did not even realize it.

The Spirit transforms us, working in us and enabling us to live the way God wills for us. And we can partner with this work by cultivating habits of gratitude.

Our habits of expressing gratitude toward God as the Creator and Sustainer of life help us keep our lives centered on God rather than on ourselves. And as the Spirit works in us, we will increasingly rejoice in the Lord always, give thanks in every circumstance, and give thanks to God in whatever we say or do.

FURTHER READING

Craig L. Blomberg, *Christians in an Age of Wealth: A Biblical Theology of Stewardship*. Grand Rapids: Zondervan, 2013.

Jacques Ellul, *Money and Power*. Eugene, OR: Wipf & Stock, 2009.

Peter Harris and Rod J. K. Wilson, *Keeping Faith in Fundraising*. Grand Rapids: Eerdmans, 2016.

Luke Timothy Johnson, *Sharing Possessions: What Faith Demands*, 2nd edition. Grand Rapids: Eerdmans, 2011.

Henri J. M. Nouwen, *A Spirituality of Fundraising*. Nashville: Upper Room, 2011.

John Stott and Christopher J. H. Wright, *The Grace of Giving: Money and the Gospel*; includes *The Gift of Accountability*. Peabody, MA: Hendrickson, 2013.

Miroslav Volf, *Giving and Forgiving in a Culture Stripped of Grace*. Grand Rapids: Zondervan, 2005.

Justin Welby, *Dethroning Mammom: Making Money Serve Grace*. London: Bloomsbury Continuum, 2016.

CONTRIBUTORS

Nicole Den Haan is principal gifts officer at Regent College.

Christie Goode is principal giving officer at Union Gospel Mission in Vancouver, BC and previously served in advancement at the University of British Columbia, Regent College, and A Rocha Canada.

Jeffrey P. Greenman is president and professor of theology and ethics at Regent College.

Stephen W. T. Stinton is capital campaign manager at Regent College.

Richard Thompson is director of advancement at Regent College.

Rod J. K. Wilson served as president of Regent College from 2000 to 2015.

www.ingramcontent.com/pod-product-compliance
Lightning Source LLC
La Vergne TN
LVHW011212080426
835508LV00007B/738

* 9 7 8 1 5 7 3 8 3 5 9 1 6 *